P9-DVD-472

M is for Money

An Economics Alphabet

Written by Debbie and Michael Shoulders and Illustrated by Marty Kelley

Economics is nothing new. Scientists believe the idea of economics—or managing resources—is about 10,000 years old. It began when the first humans settled in one place to grow crops. Prior to that, for nearly two million years, people survived as hunters and gatherers. These nomads moved often from one place to another in search of wild plants and animals to eat. When they accumulated an abundance of food they were able to settle down.

Since he no longer had to spend his time finding food, early man turned to growing food. This led to larger farms that could grow more crops. The ability to produce an abundance of resources—in this case, food—was necessary for the beginning of an economy. Hunters and gatherers still exist in the world today, but they are very few in number.

A is for Abundance

If you grow a plentiful crop,
more than you'll ever need,
Your abundance can be traded
for meat, or tools, or feed.

B is for Build

Being a successful farmer
means a family need not roam.
They can settle in one spot
and build a permanent home.

When the early people no longer lived as nomads, they found it necessary to find more permanent shelters. Using natural resources like clay, earth, stone, and wood, they built lodgings. In addition to homes they also built markets and temples. The more structures that were built in one place, the more people wanted to stay and live in that place. These permanent settlements helped early economies to grow as people traded for the food, goods, and services they needed to survive.

As the number of permanent buildings grew in one location, a civilization formed. Civilizations are groups of people known for their unique culture or lifestyle. One of the earliest examples of this was Mesopotamia—called the "cradle of civilization." Mesopotamia developed more than six thousand years ago. When the people in a civilization could count on food from farms and markets they had extra time that allowed them to pursue other activities, like art, music, and sports. It was these things that made a civilization unique.

Civilizations helped to develop the idea of "division of labor." More people living in one area let individuals focus on specialized jobs such as carpentry, bricklaying, or shopkeeping.

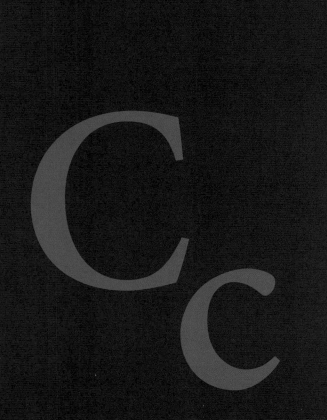

C is for Civilization

When many families come together
in one common place
they create a civilization
by sharing their lives and space.

D is for Demand and Supply

If there is not enough of something
they say the supply is low.
This creates high demand for it
and its cost will likely grow.

THE LAST
CUPCAKE$
$10

When the people in a civilization produced a surplus of resources, more items than any one family could use, they began bartering or trading those items. A chicken farmer might trade for a bushel of corn or a sack of beans—this way everyone gets the supplies they need.

Conditions like weather, insects, or diseases can harm a farmer's crops or animals. This causes their supply to decrease and means they won't have as much to barter or sell.

But people still need these things. If the supply of corn is lower than normal, the demand is high. Prices might be raised on items that are in high demand. People are willing to spend more for those resources.

If the weather is good, the insects few, and the crops healthy, a surplus exists. People can find plenty of those same beans, or eggs, or bushels of apples in the marketplace. When the supply is high, demand goes down. And the cost for those items usually drops as well.

Dd

E is for Economics

Economics is the study of how
we get things we want and need,
    how we make and swap for goods, and
why businesses fail or succeed.

Daruka

MILK

Simone

What, then, is economics? In general, people need food, shelter, and clothing. In a successful civilization people work together to make sure these items are available to everyone, but sometimes that does not happen.

Economics is the system of how people obtain the resources they need. In an economic system, the people work together to ensure fairness in the ways goods and services are produced and distributed. Usually laws are needed to protect suppliers and buyers. A stable economic system forms when people work hard for the benefits they earn, trade is encouraged, and the laws of trade are honored.

Ff

F is for Free Markets

Free market means that you decide
what to make, grow, or sell.
Buyers, if they like what you have,
will help your business excel.

Free markets provide a way for an even exchange of goods or services based on supply and demand. It's important in a free market for governments to have laws that make sure the sellers and buyers are treated fairly.

Today people sell lots of different things such as toys, clothing, and food. Sellers want to receive a fair payment for items sold to cover the cost of production. If the buyer does not pay a fair price, the seller makes no money. To prevent that from happening there are laws that protect the seller.

On the other hand, buyers want to be sure that the items they are purchasing are worth the purchase price. If a seller charges a high rate for a low-quality product, the buyer loses money. So there are laws to protect the buyer too.

People believe that in societies where free markets are encouraged, if a person works hard enough they will be able to earn extra money. Free markets offer opportunities for citizens.

Goods are the products that people grow or make to either trade or sell for money. There are some goods that all people need to have, like food and shelter. Goods are also things people buy for fun, like computers or video games.

Services are activities that people provide to others. Society needs important services like nursing, teaching, or repair work. There are also services that make life easier. Hair care, housecleaning, dog walking, and providing lawn care are some examples of services that can make life more enjoyable.

Sellers understand that they must be aware of what types of goods or services people are looking for. They also try to predict which ones will be in demand. A savvy seller can guess that when the temperature rises in the summer, the demand for ice cream will also rise.

Sellers are also in competition with anyone else who sells or provides the same thing. Competition forces sellers to figure out ways to convince buyers to choose their product over others. This might include sales or specials. These incentives help a buyer to choose which seller to visit.

Gg

G is for Goods and Services

Goods are things like ice cream cones, skateboards, bikes, or purses.
Services are provided by people: teachers, firemen, or nurses.

H is for the Housing Market

Housing markets are affected by
building materials and supplies,
the house's location, the land it's on,
and of course, its size.

Everyone needs a home, but not everyone can afford to buy a house. Those who can have many choices. People often look at several houses before making a purchase. When it comes time to make a decision, buyers ask themselves a number of questions: Can I afford the price of the house? Is it located in a neighborhood in which I want to live? Will I easily be able to sell the house when I no longer want it? This is the buyer's side of the housing market.

When builders build more houses than people in the area need, or can afford to buy, a surplus exists. This is referred to as a housing glut or buyer's market. With too many houses for sale, the builders often lower their prices in order to sell their homes. In an area where builders are concerned about abundance, they may build fewer houses. A scarcity of affordable houses creates a situation called a seller's market. Because houses are in high demand in a seller's market, the seller can better control the cost.

In a stable economy, people find ways to obtain the goods and services they need. Income is money, received over a stretch of time. It may be earned by providing a service, like dog-walking, or producing a product, like lemonade.

The money one receives through their income is usually spent to pay for the goods and services a family needs. One way to make sure that an income provides enough money is to create a budget, or a plan that shows how and where money can be spent. A useful budget includes the money needed for the family's needs and wants, money they might wish to share or donate, and some money that is set aside for future expenses or investments. Investments are things you buy now because they might be worth more in the future.

I is for Income

Income is when you get money,
usually for work you do.
It can also be from selling things
or money that's given to you.

J is for Jobs

A job is what you do for money,
like a lemonade stand or mowing.
Babysitting, walking dogs,
and even earthworm-growing.

ICE COLD LEMONADE
AND
FARM FRESH FREE RANGE
WORM

Have you ever been asked what you would like to do when you grow up? Most likely you will change your mind many times, but at some point in your life you will need to have a job. Having a job will help you earn an income.

Some common forms of employment are doctors, farmers, lawyers, salespeople, and teachers. In a world of seven billion people there are many different types of jobs. Did you know that within the medical field there are specialists whose job it is to focus on why people can't sleep? Odor testers smell underarms to make sure deodorants are performing as advertised. A wrinkle chaser is a person who irons out the wrinkles of shoe material so that there are no bumps in your footwear. One of the most well-paid jobs in the world is crab fisherman!

In the United States, child labor laws established by the Fair Labor Standards Act (FLSA) say that 14 is the minimum age you can begin work at a place of business. Younger kids who want to earn money might babysit, mow lawns, or take care of pets.

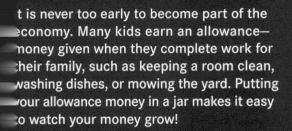

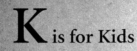 K is for Kids

Yes, kids can help the economy.
Collect allowances, and in turn,
buy some music, see a movie,
spend some of the money you earn.

It is never too early to become part of the economy. Many kids earn an allowance—money given when they complete work for their family, such as keeping a room clean, washing dishes, or mowing the yard. Putting your allowance money in a jar makes it easy to watch your money grow!

An allowance gives kids choices: Kids can save their money to purchase something that costs a lot, such as bicycle, skateboard, or a special piece of clothing. They can also choose to save part of the money for a donation; this could be to a church, a pet shelter, or any other charitable organization. But it is always fun to spend some of the allowance right away to go to the movies or out for pizza!

But remember, if you spend your allowance on movie tickets with friends, it will take you longer to buy the skateboard. You will have to decide which is more important.

If you don't receive an allowance, ask your parents if you can become part of the family economy. But you have to be ready to earn it!

There are times when money is needed for unexpected things like repair work, medical procedures, or to buy expensive items like cars and homes. If money is not readily available, the person might go to a bank and borrow money. This is called a loan because the money is only being borrowed—it will have to be paid back. The bank determines the amount of money it will loan to the borrower. This is called issuing credit. The borrower then has a debt. A debt is the amount of money owed to the bank.

In order for banks to make money they charge interest on the loan. Interest is the money a borrower pays the bank for the convenience of receiving the loan. The borrower must pay back the amount of the loan, plus the bank's interest. The percentage of interest, referred to as the interest rate, rises and falls. Low interest rates encourage people to apply for loans for the things they want to buy right now, instead of saving their money for those items. The reverse is also true; when interest rates are high, people will save up for a big purchase rather than ask for a loan.

Ll

L is for Loan

If you're running low on money
and need a little bit more,
a sister might help you with a loan
to get what you adore.

M is for Money

Money goes by many names:
dollar, shilling, peso,
franc, koruna, rupee, pound,
cabbage, yen, and euro.

In ancient times people traded goods for whatever was wanted or needed. This was called a barter economy. What happens, though, when you need something but don't have anything to trade for it? The idea of money was developed as a standard for buying. The money for an item represented what the seller and buyer agreed on as its value. Early civilizations used barley, shells, and even feathers as money. In the United States, money today consists of a combination of paper and coins controlled by the Federal Reserve System, the central bank of the United States.

Most people keep their money in a bank by setting up a bank account. Banks are businesses that offer their customers a place to save their money or borrow money if they need a loan.

M
m

N is for Needs and Wants

"Needs" are things we have to have:
        bread, shoes, doctors, and a home.
"Wants" make life more fun to live:
        pets, TV, and a cellular phone.

Let's review the definition of economics: it is the way people obtain items that may be scarce or in-demand. These items can be placed into two categories: needs and wants. People need food, shelter, health care, clothing, and a form of transportation, among other things. They will usually pay whatever is demanded for those items because without them daily life can be impossible, or at least very challenging. On the other hand, wants are things we don't need but that increase our enjoyment of life. People want cell phones, computers, video games, pets, vacations—the list of wants can go on forever! These are things that make everyday life fun. But because people must pay for their needs first, suppliers must price want items at an amount that people can afford. When you make good economic decisions you can create a balance of needs and wants.

O is for Oligopoly

Oligopolies exist when only a few companies compete.
For instance, only four companies make most of the cereals we eat.

In a free market the objective is to have even, or fair, trade. For example, when people buy shoes, they are able to choose between many different brands of shoes at a range of prices.

In an oligopoly, sales of a specific type of product are limited to only a few companies and the buyer must pay whatever those companies think is fair. If you need shoes, there are only a couple brands of shoes. Your options are limited and sellers can charge a higher price. In an oligopoly the seller has the power in the trade. In the United States, car, fuel, and steel companies enjoy an oligopoly.

Pp

P is for Producers and Consumers

Producers make the things we want:
like a cool electronic device.
Consumers, if they like the thing,
may buy it at the right price.

An economy requires producers and consumers. A producer creates a product or provides a service that people need or want. A consumer purchases those products or uses the services. People are not limited to just one role. A baker may be a producer, creating sticky buns to sell in a bakery. But when he buys the flour, sugar, and butter to produce the sticky buns, he turns into a consumer. A consumer may purchase diapers, toys, and applesauce, but when she babysits young children she becomes a producer. The intertwined relationship between producer and consumer is referred to as circular flow.

A basic rule of economics is that there are not enough resources for all the people who need them. This is referred to as scarcity. Sometimes when scarcity occurs through dire conditions like earthquakes, hurricanes, or other disasters, governments put quotas in place. When an item is put on quota, regardless of how much money a consumer has, he or she may only purchase the number of those items determined by the government. For example, when Hurricane Katrina brought floods to Louisiana, the state rationed fuel and bottled water so there would be enough of those necessities for everyone.

Another way that quotas affect the economy is through international trade. The United States may insist on quotas for products imported from another country. A German car company may only be allowed to import a certain number of cars to America each year. This keeps companies outside the United States from flooding the market with their products.

Q is for Quota

When a disaster strikes a state
and hurts their water supply
the government may set a water quota
on how much people can buy.

Everything that is made requires resources, those items that go into making the product. Resources are categorized as natural, human, or capital resources. The earth provides natural resources in the form of water, soil, plants, and minerals. Human resources are the workers who construct or create something; this might be something as large as a skyscraper or as small as a jelly bean. Human resources also include those people who provide services. Capital resources are goods that are made to produce other products. Parts that are produced in factories to eventually become cell phones, computers, or cars are examples of capital resources.

Resources are either renewable or non-renewable. Renewable resources can be maintained over a period of time. Water, soil, trees, plants, and animals will likely be available as long as people take care of them (this is why you're reminded to Reduce, Reuse, and Recycle!). Gasoline for cars and trucks is an example of a nonrenewable resource; it can't be created whenever it is needed. Conservation of nonrenewable resources is important because demand for those resources is high but supplies are limited.

R is for Resources

Resources are used to make things,
like trees to make a book.
Resources are also service people
like a reporter, repairman, or cook.

S is for Spending

Money makes the world go 'round.
Everybody loves to spend.
Without our cash and credit cards
the economy grinds to an end.

Spending money to purchase goods or services is a good thing for the economy—if you have the money. Spending allows you to buy the things you need and—as your budget allows—those things you want. Spending also ensures that the people producing goods or providing a service receive an income.

If spending money is limited, a credit card may be used. Like banks, credit cards charge interest. The credit must be paid back over time in addition to the interest. Typically a credit card company receives a payment each month. If credit cards are not paid off, the spender goes into debt. It's best to limit your debt and spending so that you have enough money for emergencies and investments.

When the prices of goods and services increase, it is called inflation. Inflation has an effect on spending. In 1920 the cost of a car was about $265 while today the average price for a car is $32,086. This is an example of inflation. Sometimes inflation happens so quickly that consumers have to stop spending because they don't have the money that the goods or services require. When inflation is high, spending goes down.

Ss

T is for Taxes

Bridges, schools, and fire trucks
are things needed every day.
Governments provide these for us
from taxes citizens pay.

T t

Governments need money for public goods and services, such things as maintaining schools, building highways, and providing safety to their citizens. One way the government gets that money is through taxes. A tax is a certain amount of money that individuals and businesses must pay to the government. Some examples are income tax—where a percentage of the money earned is sent to the government, and sales tax—paid when you purchase items. The percentages you pay are based on what you earn through income (income tax) and/or spend (sales tax). The higher the income earned or money spent, the higher the taxes paid. Families must include the taxes they will pay in their budgets.

U u

U is for United States Department of Labor

Workers in America might
work in dangerous sites
if the U.S. Department of Labor
weren't there to protect their rights.

The United States Department of Labor is a government agency that oversees the nation's workers. The agency is concerned with employment conditions and making sure that there are laws in place that protect workers. These laws focus on the hours that wage earners may work, the wages they might earn, and safety at the job.

When a wage earner encounters a situation where they are unable to work, the Department of Labor can help with unemployment wages and insurance. They also keep statistics about earning and spending in the United States. The future of our economy is influenced by the way this government agency makes and maintains laws that help wage earners.

When a good or service is ready to be sold, the seller determines its value and sets a price for it. This is the amount of money that will be paid by the consumer. The value of an item is the item's worth in money, but several things must be considered in determining the value. What did the product or service cost to produce? And what will people pay? A farmer might use milk from his cows to produce cheese to sell. The farmer considers: How much money does it cost to feed and shelter the cows? How much time did it take the farmer to make the cheese? And what did it cost to package the cheese for sale? After figuring out all of these factors, the farmer must still decide what consumers will pay for the cheese. If the farmer prices the cheese too high, then the cheese will not sell. If the price is too low, the farmer might not make a profit. Profit is money that is left over for the farmer after all of the production costs. The just-right-price becomes the value of the cheese.

V is for Value

If go-cart rides are $100
        you probably will say "NO!"
But if its value is set at $2
        you're more likely to give it a go.

W is for World Trade

People all around the world trade
for products that others make:
Japanese electronics, German cars,
and tasty Swiss chocolate cake.

Successful economies are interdependent: they need each other. Producers and consumers rely not only on their own country for goods and services but on other countries as well. World trade is an example of this interdependence.

The United States trades with many other nations in the world. Trade is grouped into two categories: imports and exports. Imports are goods and services that the U.S. buys from other countries. Exports are the goods and services that the U.S. sells to other countries.

The top three imports for the United States are cars, computers, and crude petroleum (oil). The top three exports are cars, refined petroleum (gasoline), and aircrafts. Notice how cars are number one on both lists? That means that consumers in the United States enjoy foreign cars but the consumers in other countries think American cars are a good buy as well.

W
W

X is for eXchange Rate

If you're thirsty while in Tokyo,
　　　　　the way you must begin
is to exchange U.S. dollar bills
　　　　　in return for Japanese yen.

The currency or money of the United States is the U.S. dollar but most countries have their own currency. For example, the yen is the currency used in Japan and one yen does not equal one dollar. In world trade, producers and consumers must use various forms of currency depending on the countries doing the trading. So when the United States trades with Japan or someone from the United States wants to vacation in Japan, the two countries must use an exchange rate. This is the ratio or relationship between two monetary values that allows one form of currency to be used for another. The exchange rate changes daily depending on such things as inflation, interest rates, and the economic stability of each nation. In 2015 one U.S. dollar would exchange for (about) 118 Japanese yen.

Yy

Y is for Yearly Economic Growth

Create a lemonade stand and then
record your sales this year.
If sales are higher next summer
your growth will be perfectly clear.

Economists look at how many goods and services are produced in a year, and compare it to the number of goods and services produced the previous year. The difference is referred to as the yearly economic growth of a country, usually expressed in percentages. Most industrial economies—those that produce goods and services, like the United States—average around 2% to 5% growth, but a fast-growing economy might grow as much as 10%.

Some of the industries that economists look at when determining the yearly economic growth are construction, housing, and manufacturing. The number of newly constructed houses might rise from 568,000 to 699,000 in a year's time. This is almost a 19% increase, helping to create a positive overall yearly economic growth.

Some businesses require very little money invested before they begin to make a profit. This is referred to as a zero profit condition. The California Gold Rush is a great example of zero profit condition. The Gold Rush began in 1848 when one lucky person discovered gold at a mine in California. This brought many people to the state hoping to get rich. The only things a person needed to invest to succeed in the Gold Rush was time, effort, and luck to locate the gold!

A zero profit condition encourages a large number of people to enter the business—like in the case of the Gold Rush. However, soon the supply reaches the demand and there is no further profit to be made. Or, in the case of the California Gold Rush, while the demand remained high, the supply of gold ran out.

Z is for Zero Profit Condition

If you make money with zero cash
one thing is certainly true.
When others see how much you've made
they'll rush to do that job, too!

Are you a princess? Kiss this enchanted frog to find out! 25¢

To Jason, Victoria, and Hannah,
our favorite economists and entrepreneurs.

Debbie and Mike

★

For Shelly and Greg; the only people I know who actually
knew everything in this book before they read it.

Marty

Text Copyright © 2015 Debbie and Michael Shoulders
Illustration Copyright © 2015 Marty Kelley

Sleeping Bear Press™
2395 South Huron Parkway, Suite 200
Ann Arbor, MI 48104
www.sleepingbearpress.com

Printed and bound in the United States.

Library of Congress Cataloging-in-Publication Data

Shoulders, Debbie.
M is for money : an economics alphabet / by Debbie Shoulders and Michael
Shoulders ; illustrated by Marty Kelley.
pages cm
ISBN 978-1-58536-817-4
1. Economics–Juvenile literature. 2. Alphabet books–Juvenile literature.
I. Shoulders, Michael. II. Kelley, Marty, illustrator. III. Title.
HB183.S56 2016
330–dc23
2015001546